100 Easy Recipes

Mauritian Cuisine

France Lennon

100 Easy Recipes

Mauritian Cuisine

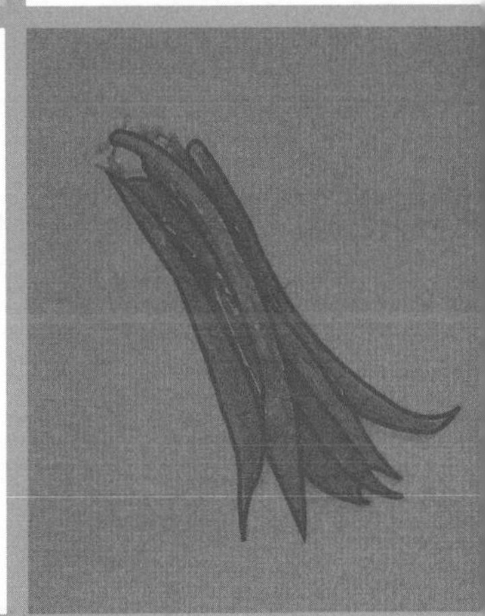

EDITIONS DE L'OCEAN INDIEN

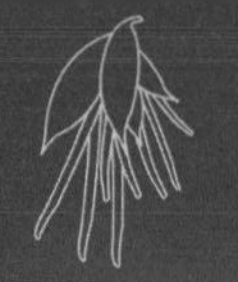

Editions de l'Océan Indien (2005)

Published by
Éditions de L'Océan Indien
Stanley, Rose-Hill, Mauritius.
Tel: 464 6761 - Fax: 464 3445
www.eoi-info.com

Layout & design: Graphic Press Ltd

1st Print : Cathay Printing Ltd (2005)
1st Reprint : SNP Security Printing Pte Ltd (2007)
2nd Reprint : T-Printers Co Ltd (2011)

ISBN 978-99903-0-493-0

Table of Contents

Unless otherwise mentioned, the recipes are for four (4) servings.

ABBREVIATIONS
tbsp: tablespoon
tsp: teaspoon
g: grams

Glossary
cotomili: coriandre : coriander
cornflour: maizena (poudre cange) : cornstarch
feuille de carri poulet: feuilles à carri : curry leaves
ourite: poulpe : octopus
safran: curcuma : turmeric
siaow: sauce de soja : soy sauce

MEASURING
1 measure of rice: 100g.

The Introduction

Nowadays, we seem not to have enough time and the last thing on one's mind is to create a proper menu. We often resort at the last minute, to the "take away" solution or end up with an unbalanced diet. It is therefore obvious that our intake of food should be improved in order not to result in lacks, deficiencies and worse illnesses.

In writing this book, I had in mind to free the housewife or househusband from anxieties. By creating weekly menus for a whole month, I have tried to lighten this load whilst giving the whole family a wide choice in our daily meals.

Some will say that this is a brilliant idea except that we need all the required ingredients at home, at the right time whenever we want to launch ourselves into action. I have therefore created a weekly list of vegetables, meat and others, which should cover each menu. That should avoid last minute hitches, which may lead you having to nip out to the "Bazaar".

I have also tried to make these menus as accessible as possible to all and I think you will agree that the dishes are neither difficult nor costly.

To begin with — before we go straight into the dishes themselves - I will explain how to make "Achards"(pickles), which complement Mauritian food so well. I will also take the opportunity to give you some other recipes, which are not included in the menus but may come in handy. Then I will go through the four monthly menus step by step.

Needless to say that you can mix and match, select the ones you prefer and those you are less fond of. However, your task will be easier if you follow the menus as they are as your shopping lists have been drawn to match each menu.

In addition to those ingredients on the lists you should have the basics such as rice, flour, salt, pepper, powdered milk, butter, sunflower oil or similar, olive oil, corn flour, cheese, whole cloves, cinnamon (ground or in sticks), mustard, vinegar, sodium bicarbonate, curry powder, breadcrumbs, soy bean sauce (Siaow), ground aniseed, sugar, bread, honey, salad cream, mayonnaise, tomato ketchup, red wine, white wine, chicken and beef stock cubes. In the hope that this book will be useful to you,

I wish you all "BON APPETIT"

"ENJOY IT"

France Lennon

The Relish

Vegetable Relish

Ingredients

1/2 lb cabbage,
1/2 lb carrots,
1/2 lb green beans,
1 tsp salt,
6 small onions,
4 garlic cloves,
4 big chillies,
2 tsp mustard grain,
1 cup oil,
2 tbsp turmeric powder,
3 tbsp vinegar.

Preparation

Shred the cabbage thinly.
Peel the carrots and cut them into small stick.
Remove the string off the green beans.
and cut them lengthwise.
Put them all in a large (non-metallic) container.
Sprinkle a tsp of salt.
Mix all and spread them on a cloth under a scorching sun, stirring from time to time.
Leave about three hours in the sun.
Cut the onion in thick wedges, crush the cloves of garlic, cut the chillies in length, crush the mustard coarsely. Heat oil in a pan.
Add the turmeric, the onions, the chillies and garlic.Stir.
Turn off fire.
Add the vegetables without washing.
Add mustard, vinegar and mix well. Correct seasoning.
Allow to cool and put in glass jar.

Mango Relish

Ingredients

5 green mangoes,
6 small onions,
4 chillies,
4 garlic cloves,
2 tsp whole mustard seeds,
2 tsp turmeric powder,
1 cup oil,
salt.

Preparation

Peel and grate the mangoes.
Press and squeeze out the juice, a handful at a time. Discard the juice.
Cut the onions and the chillies.
Crush the cloves of garlic.
Crush the mustard coarsely.
Heat oil in a pan, add onions, turmeric, crushed garlic and salt.
Turn off the fire; add the grated mangoes and the mustard.
Mix well.
Allow to cool. Put in non-metallic jars to store.

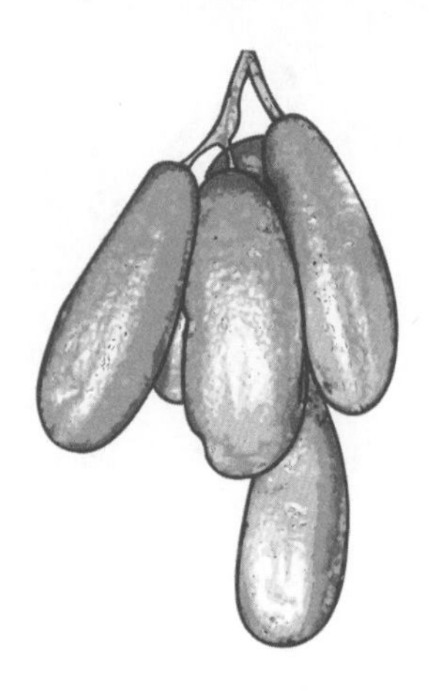

"Bilimbis Long" Relish

Ingredients

1 lb bilimbis longs
2 tbsp salt
4 tbsp sugar
5 garlic cloves
4 chillies
1 cup oil
3 tsp turmeric
2 tsp mustard seeds

Preparation

Cut the bilimbis in two lengthwise. Put them in a container covered with water. Add salt, sugar and let them soak all night.
The following day, drain the water and put the bilimbi to dry up in the sun in a large container for a few hours. Crush the garlic and chillies.
Heat oil in pan.
Add the turmeric powder, garlic and crushed chillies, the bilimbi and the mustard.
Allow to cool down before putting in jar.

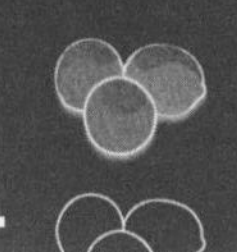

Lime Relish

Ingredients

15 limes of Rodrigues
10 small green chillies
1 cup oil
2 tbsp turmeric powder
5 cloves crushed garlic
2 tsp mustard seeds
salt

Preparation

Boil the lemons in lightly salted water for 5 minutes.
Allow to cool. Reserve the cooking water.
Leave to macerate in a jar (non-metallic) for 15 days.
After 15 days, take them out of the jar, remove the seeds and cut them into small pieces.
Remove the stalk from the chillies.
Crush the mustard.
Heat oil in pan till very hot.
Turn off heat. Put the turmeric, garlic, the chillies, the pieces of lemon and the mustard.
Stir and cool down before putting back in jar.

Olives Relish

Ingredients

2 lbs green olive
salt
3 tsp turmeric powder
4 garlic cloves
2 tsp mustard grains
1 cup oil

Preparation

Bring half pan of water to boil. Fill pan to half with water. Bring to boil.
Add the olives and salt.
Turn off the heat and allow to cool.
Put olives in a jar for 10 days.
Prepare exactly as for the bilimbi. (P. 10)

The Soup

Watercress soup

Ingredients

2 bunch watercress
2 big potatoes
1 onion
1 tbsp cornstarch
1 tbsp powdered milk
1/2 tbsp butter
salt to taste

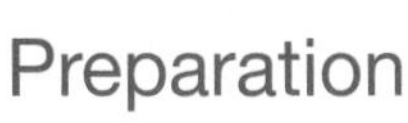

Preparation

Clean the watercress.
Peel potatoes, wash and boil with the watercress
and salt in 1 litre of water in a pressure pan for about 15 minutes.
Cool and blend them all.
Mix the cornstarch and the milk powder with water.
Heat butter in a saucepan with chopped onion and pour the blended vegetables.
Add the mixture of the cornstarch / milk.
As soon as the soup starts to thicken, remove from heat. Serve hot.

Corn soup

Ingredients

1 can of sweetcorn cream
1 tbsp cornstarch
1 tbsp powdered milk
1 tbsp butter
2 tbsp grated cheese
salt at will

Preparation

Sieve the sweetcorn cream.
Stir with a large spoon, add 2 tbsp of water from time to time, till there's nothing in the sieve.
Add 3 cups of water.
Put the sweetcorn cream in a saucepan and bring to boil.
Mix the cornstarch and milk with half-cup of water and add to sweetcorn.
Add butter and let it boil for 3 minutes.
Add the grated cheese. Season.
Serve very hot.

Onion soup

Ingredients

3 Bombay onions
1 tbsp cornstarch
1 tbsp milk
1 large spoon butter
salt to taste, a small slice of cheese "tete de maure"(Edam cheese).

For the croutons:
4 slices of stale bread
oil

Preparation

Melt butter in a pressure cooker.
Add the chopped onions until it changes colour, stirring continuously.
Add 6 cups water, salt and cover the pressure cooker.
Let it cook for 15 minutes, and as soon as the hissing sound starts, switch off heat. Allow the pressure to drop without opening. Then open the pressure cooker.
Blend the content.
Mix the cornstarch and milk with a cup of water.
Bring the soup to boil again and add the mixture of cornstarch/milk.
Let it boil for 3 seconds.
Switch off heat.

Prepare the croutons:
Cut bread into cubes and fry them in very hot oil until evenly browned but not burnt.
Serve the soup very hot with the grated cheese and the croutons.

Vegetable soup with chicken or beef

Ingredients

1/2 lb pumpkin
2 carrots
1 'chou-chou'
1 leek
1 stem celery
1 tomato
1 onion
1 potato
spring onions
salt at will
one chicken or beef stock cube
125 g beef or a carcass of chicken.

Preparation

Clean the piece of beef or chicken, removing all the fat and the skin.
Peel all the vegetables, onion and cut them in pieces.
Put them all in a pressure cooker with the piece of beef or chicken carcass.
Add 1 litre of water and let them cook for about half an hour.
When the vegetables are well cooked, remove the chicken carcass and blend them.
Put on fire and let cook for 5 minutes. Add the chicken or beef stock cube.
Serve very hot with crusty bread and butter.

The Faratas

Faratas

Ingredients

1 1/2 lbs of flour, 1 1/2 tsp of salt, 1 1/2 cup water, 3 tbsp oil.

Preparation

Put the flour in a mixing bowl
and add salt.
Add one cup of water.
Knead the dough till it becomes
smooth, add more water if necessary.
Cut the dough in small pieces.
Knead again.
Repeat the process several times.
If the dough is too soft,
sprinkle with some flour.
Make balls of approximately 75 grams.
Flatten each ball with a rolling pin to
give it the circular shape of the "tawa"
(griddle).
Put some oil in a bowl.
Soak a piece of cloth in the oil
and spread it on the surface of the
dough.
Fold the dough in four to make
it become square.
Repeat the exercise with all the balls
to obtain 20 squares.
Then roll out the small dough again
and flatten them with the rolling pin.
Put the "tawa" on a hot plate
and let warm up for 10 minutes.
Put a flattened farata on the hot plate,
leave it a few seconds and turn it with
a knife.
Oil the farata on each side.
When the farata is ready, remove from
the tawa, fold it, keep covered to
remain hot.
Do the same thing for all
the other prepared dough.

The Vindayes

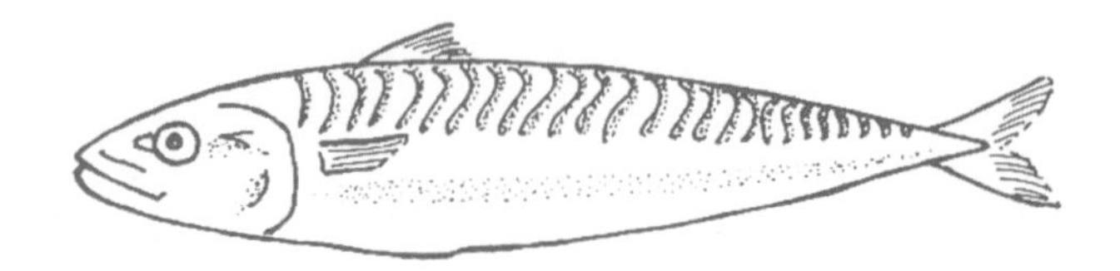

Fish vindaye

Ingredients

1 kg fish "Vacoas or Sacré-chien"
10 small onions
5 garlic cloves
4 whole chillies
2 tsp crushed mustard seeds
2 tsp turmeric powder
2 tsp vinegar
salt
1 cup oil

Preparation

Cut the fillet of fish in slices, fry them in hot oil and keep aside.
Heat oil in a pan.
Turn off heat and put all ingredients in the pan.
Allow to cool down before adding fish slices.
Do not stir with a spoon but shake the saucepan from time to time to allow the ingredients to mix properly with the fish.

Note: The vindaye does not keep for a long time. It is advisable to make vindaye in small quantities and consumed as soon as possible.

Octopus Vindaye

Ingredients

1 1/2 kg clean octopus
10 small onions
5 garlic cloves
4 whole chillies
2 tsp crushed mustard
2 tsp turmeric powder
2 tsp vinegar
1 cup oil

Preparation

Boil the octopus for about 45 minutes in a pressure cooker.
Open and see if it is done, i.e fairly soft, otherwise add more water and let cook for about 15 minutes.
Remove from heat and allow to cool completely.
Cut in small pieces and keep aside.
Put oil to warm the octopus in a saucepan.
Switch off heat and put all ingredients except the octopus in the oil. Allow to cool before adding the octopus. Do not stir with a spoon, but shake the saucepan from time to time to allow the ingredients to mix properly with the pieces of octopus.

Note: The vindaye does not keep for a long time. It is advisable to make vindaye in small quantities and consumed as soon as possible.

Accommodated Rice

Pilau (See P62)

Spanish Rice (See P49)

Khichri

Ingredients

2 1/2 measures of rice
1/2 measure of red lentils
1 tbsp butter (or ghee)
1 tsp cumin powder
1 big onion
3 garlic cloves
1 bunch coriander leaves, 2 tbsp oil
salt.

Preparation

Put oil and butter to warm in a saucepan.
Add the sliced onion, the crushed garlic, the cumin powder and the red lentils.
Cook for about 15 minutes.
Wash the rice and put in the rice cooker.
Pour the preparation of lentil on it.
Add 3 measures* of water and let cook.
When the cooking is over, sprinkle the chopped coriander.

* the same measurement used for the rice.

Cantonese Rice

Ingredients

2 1/2 measures rice
2 eggs
1 chicken's breast
1/2 can of Chinese sausage (optional)
2 carrots
1/4 cabbage
5 to 6 tbsp soy sauce
1 tsp sugar
3 garlic cloves
1 bunch coriander leaves
1 bunch spring onion
oil, salt, pepper.

Preparation

Boil the rice with plenty of water till the rice is half cooked.
Drain and allow to cool.
Cut chicken into strips.
Marinate in one tbsp of oil, soy sauce, garlic thinly cut, pepper, sugar and a pinch of salt.
Peel and grate the carrots. Thinly shred the cabbage (optional).
Make an omelet with the eggs and cut them in strips.
Put 2 tbsp of oil to warm in a wok on a burning hot fire.
Add the marinade chicken and stir fry for 5 minutes.
Add the thinly sliced chinese sausage. Add the rice a little at a time, together with a little soy sauce and some vegetables. Continue until all the vegetables and rice are used up.
Pour all the preparation in the rice cooker.
Add the coriander, the chopped onion spring and omelet.
Cover and switch on the rice cooker.

Briani (easy)*

Ingredients

2 1/2 measures rice
750 g beef
1 plain yoghurt
8 small potatoes
4 white onions
2 tsp cumin powder
8 garlic cloves
1 piece ginger
1 bunch coriander
1 bunch mint
1/4 sachet Briani spices
1/4 cup oil
1 pinch orange coloured powder
salt

Preparation

Cut the meat in cubes.
Marinate overnight with the yoghurt, 1 chopped onion, 2 tbsp oil, mint and chopped coriander, briani spices, cumin, garlic, crushed ginger, orange coloured powder and salt. Place in the fridge.
Boil the rice with plenty of water till rice is half cooked. Drain and cool down.
Cut the potato in large pieces and half fry.
Fry the meat for about 25 minutes.
Place at the bottom of the rice cooker a layer of white rice, then a layer of onions, potatoes, meat and repeat with the rice etc till nothing is left.
Switch on the rice cooker and let cook.
When the cooking is over, sprinkle the chopped coriander.

* This is an easy preparation to do rather than the traditional Briani.

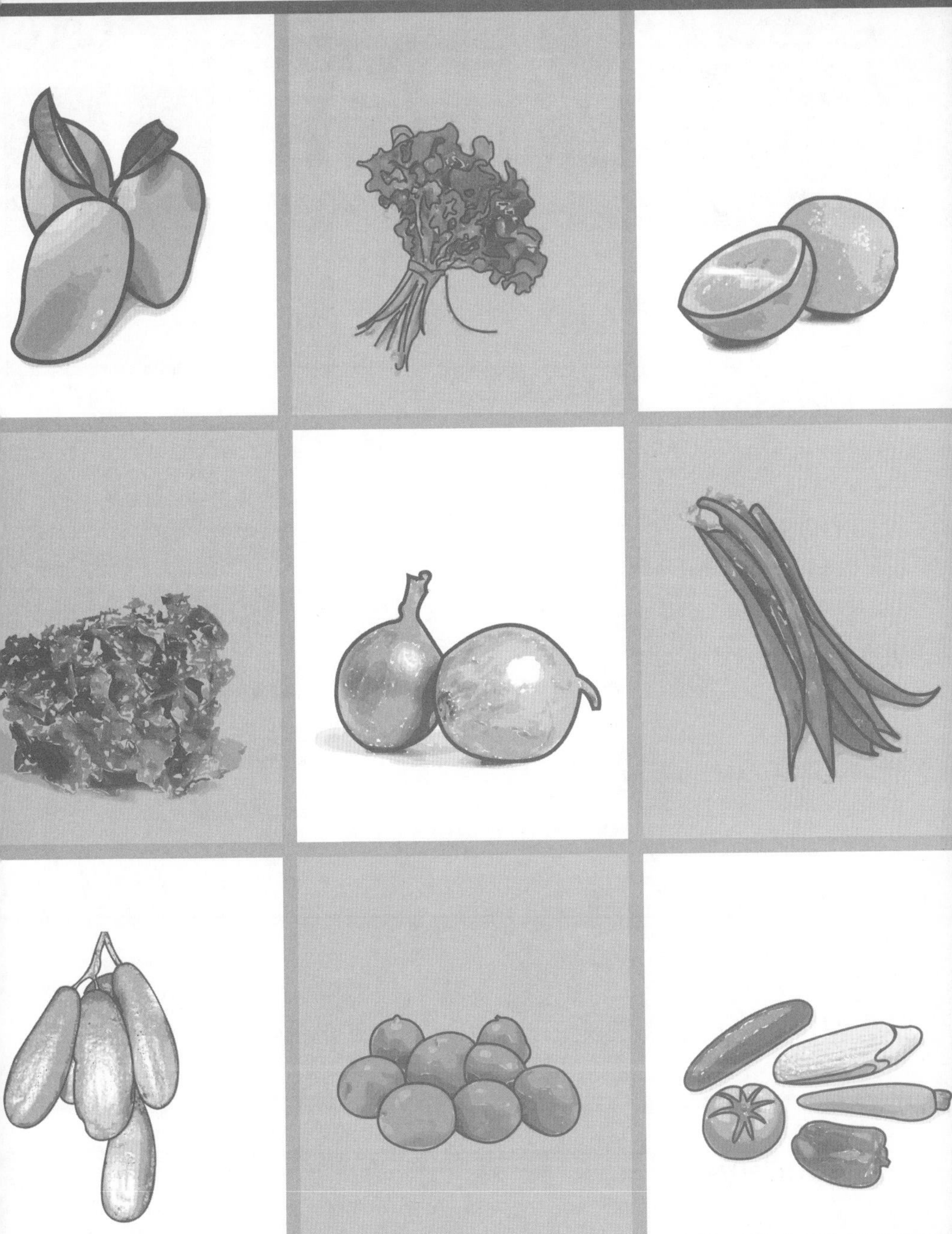

Menu 1

	Morning	Evening
Monday	Fricassee of "chou chou". Egg with tomato sauce.	Tuna soufflé. Breaded egg-plant. Watercress salad.
Tuesday	Braised cabbage with sausage. Coriander chutney.	Fried meat "Chinese style". Gratin of pumpkin. Lettuce salad.
Wednesday	Fricassee of black lentils. Snoek with tomato sauce. Endives chutney.	Pâtissons stuffed with chicken. Lettuce salad.
Thursday	Watercress "bouillon". Beef daube. Potato chutney.	Spinach and ham quiche. Mixed salad.
Friday	Brèdes songes. (Taro leaves) Sardines in tomato sauce.	Macaroni with chopped meat or corned beef. Watercress salad.
Saturday	"Patoles" fricassee. Dried shrimps with tomato sauce. Egg-plant chutney.	Grilled meat. Jacket baked potatoes. Mixed salad. Rice salad.
Sunday	Chicken curry. Tomato chutney.	Breaded fish fillet. Pipengailles cooked in milk. Lettuce salad.

The purchase list

Market

750 g 'chou chou'
1 kg pumpkin
2 big egg-plant (about 3/4 lb)
1 cabbage
3 endives
5 pâtissons (squash)
2 kg potatoes
500 g spinach
1 cucumber

3 bunches brèdes songes (taro leaves)
1 kg patoles (snake gourd)
250 g egg-plant
1.5 kg pipengailles
5 lettuces
7 bunches watercress
1 kg onions
1.5 kg tomatoes

125 g garlic
125 g ginger
125 g turmeric
1 bunch parsley
1 bunch thyme
3 bunches coriander
1 bunch shallot

Supermarket

Green chilli
1 sprig of carri poulé (curry leaves)
2 green apples
2 small can of tomatoes purée
250 g black lentils
1 can of tuna flakes in brine
1 can sweetcorn
2 cans of sardines in oil
1 x 250 g carton 'cheddar'
1 jar green olive (pickled and stoned)

1 can corned beef or
1 tray of minced meat
1 tray chicken of your choice
1 chicken (whole)
1 tray of minced chicken or chicken breast
1 packet (500g) sausage (pork or chicken)
Pork or lamb chops
1 packet of fish fillet

3 slices of ham
1 kg beef
250 g cocktail sausages
1 piece of cheese "Gruyere"
125 g salted fish (snoek)
125 g dried shrimps
1 packet of macaroni (500g)
15 eggs
1 lemon

MORNING

Fricassée of “chou chou”

Ingredients

750 g of ‘chou chou’, 1 tbsp oil, 1 small onion,

1 crushed garlic clove, salt to taste, 1 bunch parsley.

Preparation Peel the chou chou, cut them in cubes and put in a saucepan. Add oil, salt, chopped onion, crushed garlic and a cup of water. Cook on gentle heat for twenty minutes. Stir from time to time to prevent sticking. When done, sprinkle with chopped parsley and switch off heat.

Egg with tomato sauce

Ingredients

2 eggs per person, 1 small onion, crushed garlic,

6 tomatoes, oil, 1 tbsp tomato purée.

Preparation Fry the eggs and place them in a plate close to each other.

Prepare the sauce: Chop onion and tomatoes. Heat oil in pan, add chopped onion, crushed garlic and the tomatoes. Cook for a while and add a little water. Simmer until tomatoes are well cooked. Add the tomato purée. Put eggs one by one in the sauce by taking care not to break them. Let cook for a few minutes and remove from heat.

EVENING

Tuna Soufflé

Ingredients

1 can of tuna flakes in water,
3 tomatoes, 1/2 onion (chopped)

For the cream:

1 tbsp butter, 1 tbsp flour, 1 egg, 1 cup milk, a small piece of cheese 'Gruyère'.

Preparation Drain water from tuna. Heat oil, add chopped onion and tomato. Add tuna flakes when tomatoes are well cooked. Cook a few minutes further. Pour mixture in an ovenproof dish. Keep aside.

Prepare the cream using the roux method: Melt butter in a saucepan. Add the flour all at once. Reduce heat. Cook for 2 minutes, stirring well. Add milk gradually, stirring continuously to prevent lumps from forming. Mix in the yolk and remove from heat. Whisk egg white until stiff, fold in gently into the cream. Pour in the cream on to the tuna sauce. Sprinkle grated cheese. Bake in preheated oven (180°C) for 10 minutes. Serve at once.

Egg-plant fritters

Ingredients

1 x 375 g egg-plant, 3 tbsp flour, salt, pepper, oil.

Preparation Prepare batter with flour, 1/2 cup water, a tbsp oil, and pepper. Mix well with a whisk until the batter is smooth (neither too liquid nor too thick). Cut the egg-plant in thin slices. Dip each slice in the batter and fry in hot oil. Let brown on one side, turn it and let brown on the other side. Repeat with other slices. Do not put more than three slices at a time.

Watercress salad

Ingredients

2 bunches watercress, 2 tbsp olive oil, 1/2 tbsp vinegar, 1/2 tsp mustard paste, salt, pepper.

Preparation Clean and wash the watercress. Mix oil, vinegar, mustard, salt, pepper to make the vinaigrette dressing. Mix the watercress and the vinaigrette just before serving.

MORNING

Braised cabbage with sausages

Ingredients

1 cabbage, 1/2 lb small creole sausages or fried chicken sausages, 1 onion, 1 tsp crushed garlic and ginger, 3 tomatoes, salt, 2 cloves, oil, coriander, 1/2 tsp of sugar.

Preparation Clean and shred the cabbage roughly. Separate the sausages. Chop onion. Warm oil in a saucepan. Add the chopped onion, garlic and ginger, the sausages and cook for a while before adding the cabbage, the whole tomatoes, the cloves and salt. Cover and simmer for twenty minutes by stirring from time to time. Add water if necessary and let cook for a few seconds more. Crush the tomatoes with a spoon and mix well. Add some chopped coriander and sugar. Switch off heat.

Coriander chutney

Ingredients

3 tomatoes, 1 bunch coriander, 2 green chillies,
1 small onion, 1 tsp of garlic, salt.

Preparation Blend all in a mixer.
Pour in a bowl to serve.

EVENING

Fried meat Chinese Style

Ingredients

500 g beef, 1 tbsp cornstarch, salt, pepper, 2 or 3 tbsp soy sauce, 1 big bombay onion (sliced into rings), 2 tbsp oil.

Preparation Cut beef into thin strips with a very sharp knife. Marinate with soy sauce, salt, pepper, cornstarch and 1 tbsp of oil. Heat 1 tbsp of oil in a wok on high heat. When the oil is very hot, add the pieces of meat and the marinade. Stir fry for 10 minutes. Add the onion rings and stir well for 5 minutes. Remove from heat.

Pumpkin au gratin

Ingredients

1 kg pumpkin, 1 onion, 1 tbsp oil, thyme, parsley, 1 tbsp butter, 1 tbsp milk powder, 1 egg yolk, 2 tbsp grated cheese (Cheddar).

Preparation Peel pumpkin, cut in small pieces and put in a saucepan with thinly chopped onion, thyme, oil and little water. Cook on low heat for 15 minutes or until tender, adding more water if necessary. Crush with a fork to obtain a purée. Add butter, milk, the egg yolk and cheese. Pour in a gratin dish, sprinkle with breadcrumbs. Brown under the grill.

Lettuce salad

Ingredients

1 lettuce, 2 tbsp olive oil, 1/2 tbsp vinegar, 1/2 tsp mustard paste, salt, pepper.

Preparation Clean and spin lettuce. Mix oil, vinegar, mustard, salt, pepper to make a vinaigrette dressing. Toss lettuce in vinaigrette just before serving.

MORNING

Black lentils

Ingredients

250 g black lentils, 1/2 chopped onion, 1 sprig thyme,
crushed garlic and ginger, salt, oil.

Preparation Clean and wash the lentil. Pressure cook with all the other ingredients. Add 6 cups of water and cook for 45 minutes. Remove from heat. Allow pressure to drop before opening pressure cooker. Serve.

Snoek (salted fish) with tomato sauce

Ingredients

125 g salted fish (snoëk), 5 tomatoes, 1/2 chopped onion, crushed garlic and ginger, oil.

Preparation Put salted fish to boil in 3 cups of water for 10 minutes. Allow to cool down. Flake fish and remove all the bones. Heat two rounds of oil in a saucepan. Fry the salted fish for a few seconds and remove from fire.

Preparing the sauce: Heat 2 tbsp oil in a saucepan. Fry chopped onions, crushed garlic and ginger and the tomatoes. Cook for a few minutes, add water if necessary. Add the salted fish and let cook a few minutes more.

Endives Chutney

Ingredients

3 endives, 1 onion (sliced into rings), salt, 2 tbsp vinegar, 2 tbsp oil.

Preparation Boil the endives in 2 cups of water. When they are tender, allow to cool down and peel them delicately. Crush them with a fork. First add the vinegar, then salt, oil and onions.

EVENING

Pâtissons (Squashes) stuffed with chicken

Ingredients

5 medium size squashes, 1 tray or 1 breast chopped chicken, 1 chopped onion, 1 sprig thyme, parsley, 2 slices from a loaf bread (a day old), 1 cup of milk, 1 tbsp oil.

Preparation Boil the whole squashes after washing them. Remove from the cooking water taking care not to break them. Make a small circular cut around the stem and remove like a hat. Scoop out the flesh with a small spoon, by taking care not to deform or crush them. Place the squash shells on a baking tray. Keep pulp aside. Heat 1 tbsp of oil in a saucepan; add the onions, chopped chicken and thyme. Cook. Add water if necessary. In the meantime, put the slices of bread to soak in milk for 3 minutes and press well to drain the water. Mix the squash pulp, pressed bread, chopped parsley and blend in a mixer. Add this preparation to the cooked chicken, cook for 10 minutes on a low heat by stirring from time to time. Fill all the squashes with the stuffing, then cover with the small hat. Bake in the oven fifteen minutes before serving.

Lettuce Salad (see P29)

MORNING

Watercress in bouillon

Ingredients

2 bunches watercress, 1/2 onion, salt, 3 cups water, 1 tsp oil.

Preparation Clean the watercress and wash with plenty of water. Heat oil in a saucepan. Add the chopped onion, salt and water. Add the watercress and let boil for 3 minutes more. Remove from heat.

Braised beef

Ingredients

500 g beef, 1 chopped onion, 1 tsp crushed garlic, pepper, salt, 1 tbsp chopped parsley, oil, 4 tomatoes chopped in small pieces, 1/2 tsp cinnamon powder, 1/2 tsp flour.

Preparation Cut beef in thin slices. Heat 2 tbsp oil in saucepan; add the onion, garlic and the meat. Let brown a little, then add pepper, salt and the tomatoes. Allow to brown a little more; add a cup of water and lower the heat. Simmer for half an hour more, adding water if necessary. Mix the cinnamon and flour with water and pour it on the meat. Let simmer a little more and remove from heat. Sprinkle the chopped parsley.

Potato chutney

Ingredients

3 potatoes, 1 onion (sliced into rings), salt, pepper,
green chillies at will (optional), 1 tbsp vinegar, 2 tbsp oil.

Preparation Boil the potatoes. Peel and mash them with a fork. Add salt and pepper, onion slices, vinegar, oil, and chopped chillies (optional). Mix all.

EVENING

Spinach and ham quiche

(The ham can be replaced by smoked chicken or smoked marlin).

Ingredients

For the pastry:

300 g flour, 125 g butter,
1 egg yolk, salt, 3 tbsp water.

For the filling:

3 slices ham, 500 g spinach, 2 large onions,
1 tbsp of butter, 1 tbsp flour, 1/2 cup milk,
2 whole eggs, 50 g grated cheese, salt, pepper.

Preparation Preparing short pastry: Rub butter into flour and salt. Add yolk and enough water to bind all ingredients together. Mix and knead lightly to form a soft, smooth dough. Roll dough on floured surface a little larger than the tart tin. Line greased tin. Prick base with a fork. Leave aside.

Preparing the garnish: Clean, boil the spinach, drain and cut thinly. Slice the onion, fry in little oil until soft, then add the spinach. Melt butter in a saucepan, add flour and milk. Beat with a whisk to prevent formation of lumps. Add onion, spinach and the chopped ham. Turn off the heat. Add the two eggs and stir very rapidly with a wooden spoon. Add salt and pepper. Allow to cool. Preheat oven at 180°C for 10 minutes. Put the filling in pastry case. Sprinkle with grated cheese and bake for 30 to 35 minutes.

Mixed salad

Ingredients

1 lettuce, 1/2 bunch watercress, 1/2 cucumber, 1/2 tin sweetcorn,
1 green apple, salt, pepper, 1/2 tsp vinegar, 1 tsp olive oil, 1 tsp mustard.

Preparation Wash the lettuce and the watercress. Peel and cut the cucumber and the apple in cubes. Drain the sweetcorn. Prepare vinaigrette with oil, vinegar, mustard, salt, and pepper. Mix all just before serving.

MORNING

Taro Leaves (Brèdes Songes)

Ingredients

3 bunches of Taro leaves, 4 tomatoes, 1 onion, 1/2 tsp crushed garlic, 1/2 tsp crushed ginger, salt, 2 tsp vinegar, 3 tbsp oil.

Preparation Cut the taro leaves in small pieces. Wash and put them in pressure pan with salt, vinegar and cover with a little water. Pressure cook for ten minutes as from the moment when the hissing sound starts. Drain. Chop onion and tomatoes. Heat oil in a saucepan. Add onion, garlic, ginger and tomatoes. Lightly fry, add the taro leaves. Cook for a few more minutes.

Sardines with tomato sauce*

Ingredients

2 cans sardines, 1 onion, 4 tomatoes, 1/2 tsp crushed garlic,
1/2 tsp crushed ginger, 3 tbsp oil.

Preparation Chop onion and tomatoes. Drain oil from sardines. Heat oil in a sauce pan. Add the chopped onion, garlic, ginger and tomatoes. Cook for 5 minutes and add the sardines without crushing them.

* The sardines can be added to the taro leaves instead of making a sauce.

EVENING

Macaroni with minced meat or corned beef

(For 6 Persons)

Ingredients

1 x 500 g packet macaroni, 500 g chopped meat or 1 can corned beef, 1 tbsp oil, 1 tbsp butter, 1 chopped onion, 1 small tin tomato purée, thyme, parsley, salt.

Preparation Bring a pan of water to boil with oil and salt. As soon as it boils, put the macaroni in it. Boil for fifteen minutes stirring from time to time. Check the cooking and drain. Melt butter in a saucepan. Add chopped onion and chopped meat or the corned beef. Brown for a few minutes and then add the tomato purée, thyme, parsley and cook until water has evaporated and meat is cooked. Check the seasoning before mixing the macaroni. Let cook for a few more minutes, stirring every now and then.

- Watercress Salad (see P27)

MORNING

Fricassée of patoles (snake gourd)

Ingredients

1 kg of patoles, 1 chopped onion, 1/2 tsp crushed garlic, 2 tsp oil,
1 pinch sodium bicarbonate, salt.

Preparation Scrape the patoles and cut them in halves lengthwise. Remove the seeds and cut in thin strips. Put in a bowl with 2 tbsp of salt and rub well with your hands till the slices of patoles become transparent. Leave in the salt for 10 minutes then wash with plenty of water. Warm oil in a sauce pan. Add the chopped onion, garlic, patoles and the sodium bicarbonate. Cover and let cook on a slow heat for about 15 minutes. Correct the seasoning.

Dry shrimps in tomato sauce

Ingredients

125 g dried shrimps, 6 chopped tomatoes, 1 chopped onion, 1/2 tsp crushed garlic,
1/2 tsp crushed ginger, 2 tbsp oil, salt.

Preparation Soak dried shrimps in warm water for 15 minutes. Wash, clean and flake them coarsely in a mincer. Heat oil in a saucepan. Add the chopped onion followed by the dried shrimps, garlic and ginger. Cook for 3 minutes, then add the tomatoes. Add water and allow to cook. Check seasoning.

5 small glasses of small river shrimps can be used. Wash them in a large strainer. Crush with the other ingredients in a mixer. Warm oil, and add the purée. Cover and let cook for 10 minutes.

Egg-plant chutney

Ingredients

1 big egg-plant, 2 tbsp oil, 2 tsp vinegar, 1 chopped onion, salt, pepper.

Preparation Boil the egg-plant. Prepare vinaigrette with oil, vinegar, onion, salt and pepper. Mix well and keep aside. When egg-plant is done and cooled down, peel it and crush with a fork. Mix the purée with the sauce.

EVENING

Grilled meat

Ingredients

1 tray of chicken pieces of your choice, 1 packet of sausage (pork or chicken), pork or lamb chops, 5 tbsp soy sauce, thyme, parsley, salt, pepper, 1 tbsp honey or sugar.

Preparation Put the chicken, meat and sausage to marinate in remaining ingredients for at least 4 hours. In the evening, light on the BBQ grill and let cook the meat or put in the oven.

Potato baked in their skins (Jacket potato)

Ingredients

2 potatoes per person.

Preparation Wash and scrub the potatoes. Wrap them in aluminium foil and put on the charcoal of the BBQ or in an oven for all the duration of the cooking of the meat.

Mixed Salad (see P33)

Rice salad

Ingredients

2 ricecooker measures of rice, 5 tbsp olive oil, juice of 1 lemon, 1 onion (sliced into rings), 6-7 pitted olives, 1/2 can sweetcorn kernels, 125 g processed cheddar cheese - cut into cubes, 1 small bunch finely chopped spring onion, 1 packet of thinly chopped shallot, salt, pepper.

Preparation Wash the rice and put in a pan of boiling water. Cook for 8 to 10 minutes, wash in plenty of water, drain and allow to cool. Mix all the ingredients in a salad bowl and pour on the rice. Shake the bowl to mix well.

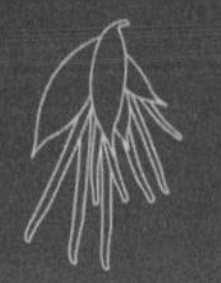

MORNING

Chicken curry

Ingredients

1 chicken, 2 young and tender egg-plants or 3 potatoes, 3 tbsp curry powder, 1 tbsp cumin powder, 1 chopped onion, 1 sprig curry leaves, 3 tomatoes, 1 bunch coriander leaves, 1/2 tsp crushed garlic, 1/2 tsp crushed ginger, salt, pepper.

Preparation Remove skin and all the visible fat from the chicken. Cut chicken into pieces. Put the chicken pieces in a saucepan with salt, pepper, chopped onion, the egg-plant cut lengthwise, or the potatoes cut in pieces, curry powder, cumin powder, chopped tomatoes, the curry leaves, garlic, ginger and water. Mix all. Cook for 30 minutes. Stir from time to time and add water if necessary. Crush the egg-plant thoroughly to thicken the sauce. When the chicken is done, sprinkle the chopped coriander.

Tomato chutney

Ingredients

5 tomatoes, 1 medium-sized onion, salt, 5 small green chillies.

Preparation Chop the tomatoes, onion and chillies. Mix all and add salt just before serving.

EVENING

Fillets of breaded fish

Ingredients

4 fish fillets, 3 tbsp flour, 5 tbsp oil, 1 sprig chopped parsley, salt, pepper.

Preparation Fry the fillets of fish. Prepare the fritter batter: mix flour, salt, pepper, parsley and blend with half cup of water to obtain a thick batter. Dip the fish fillet one by one in the batter and fry them in very hot oil.

Pipengailles (ridged gourd) with milk

Ingredients

1.5 kg pipengailles, 1 tbsp oil, 1 chopped onion, 1 branch thyme, salt, 1 tbsp butter, 1 tbsp flour, 1/2 cup milk, 1 egg yolk, breadcrumb.

Preparation Peel the pipengailles, cut in slices and put them in a saucepan with oil, chopped onion, thyme and salt. Cook for 15 minutes by stirring from time to time. Remove from fire when tender, cool and reduce into a puree in a mixer. Melt butter in saucepan. Add all the flour and stir with a wooden spoon. Add milk little at a time, stirring well to prevent lumps formation. Add the yolk and the purée of pipengaille. Mix well. Pour in a baking dish. Sprinkle with breadcrumb and grill just before serving.

Lettuce Salad (see P29)

Menu 2

	Morning	Evening
Monday	Chicken moulouctany. Coconut chutney.	Beef with wine. Sauteed green beans. Lettuce salad.
Tuesday	Curry of calebasse with dried shrimps. Cucumber salad.	Roast chicken. Courgettes in white sauce.
Wednesday	Red lentil. Braised fish. Fried margozes (Bittergourd)	Moussaka. Lettuce salad.
Thursday	Chicken chop suey. Tomato chutney.	Gratin of potatoes and cod. Cabbage salad.
Friday	Fricassee of pumpkin. Tuna in tomato sauce. Fried egg-plant.	Spanish rice. Tomato chutney.
Saturday	Bouillon of brède giraumon (pumpkin leaves) Meat in tomato sauce. Mango chutney.	Raw vegetable salad with smoked marlin and the croutons. Garlic bread.
Sunday	Curry of pork and egg-plant. Cucumber salad.	Vegetable soup with chicken or beef. Chicken stuffed bread.

The purchase list

Market

Small green chillies
Onions
500 g green beans
1 tender calebasse
1 courgette
500 g margozes (bittergourd)
1 kg medium egg-plant
250 g carrots
250 g chou-chou
1 radish
250 g chinese brède
1 kg potatoes
1 medium cabbage
1 kg pumpkin

1 big egg-plant
500 g small egg-plant
2 bunches pumpkin greens
2 green mangoes
1 bunch watercress
125 g sprouted moong beans
2 cucumbers
3 lettuces
125 g garlic
125 g ginger
1.5 kg of tomatoes
3 sprigs curry leaves
4 bunches coriander
1 bunch mint

2 pieces coconut
thyme
parsley
1 green apple
1 avocado

For the soup:
1 leek
1 stem celery
Spring onion

For stuffed bread :
1 lettuce
2 tomatoes

Supermarket

1 packet processed cheese "Cheddar" (500g)
2 whole chicken
1 tray chicken of your choice
500 g breast chicken
1 kg beef
1 x 500g pkt chopped meat
1 kg pork
4 slices of fish

1 packet of smoked marlin (500g)
125 g dry shrimps
125 g cod
1 small tin chinese sausage
1 can of tuna in brine
1 small tin tomato purée
1 can sweetcorn kernels
1 pkt of green olives (pitted)
6 eggs

1 packet of red lentil (500g)
1 packet of dholl "embrevades" (500g)
1 sachet of Moulouctany mix
For the vegetable soup:
1 carcass chicken
For the stuffed bread:
2 chicken breast
250 g pumpkin
2 carrots
1 chou-chou

MORNING

Chicken Moulouctany

Ingredients

1 tray chicken of your choice, 1/4 cup of peas "embrevade", 200 g "moulouctany" mix, 1 chopped onion, 1/2 tsp crushed garlic, 1/2 tsp crushed ginger, 4 chopped tomatoes, 1 sprig curry leaves, 1 tbsp oil, salt, 1 bunch of coriander.

Preparation Put chicken, peas and salt in a pressure cooker with 6 cups of water. Pressure cook for half an hour as from the hissing sound. When the peas are done, heat oil in a saucepan. Add the chopped onion, garlic, ginger, tomatoes, curry leaves and the "moulouctany" mix. Allow to cook for 2 minutes, then add the peas and the chicken. Check seasoning. Sprinkle the finely chopped coriander.

Coconut chutney

Ingredients

2 pieces of coconut, 1/2 onion, salt, 5 curry leaves, 5 sprigs mint, 1 gherkin or some tamarind or 1 slice of green mango or 1 olive (whatever is available), chillies (optional).

Preparation Cut the coconut in small pieces or grate it. Put all the ingredients in a mincer and crush them adding some water.

EVENING

Beef braised in wine

Ingredients

500 g of beef, 1 tsp thyme, 1 tbsp chopped parsley, salt, pepper, 2 crushed garlic cloves, 1/2 tsp cinnamon powder, 1 onion (sliced into rings), 4 crushed tomatoes, 2 tbsp tomato sauce (ketchup), 1 tsp flour, 1/2 glass red wine, 1/2 tsp of sugar, 3 tbsp of oil.

Preparation Cut the meat in small cubes and marinate for 1 hour with the thyme, parsley, 1 tbsp oil, 5 tbsp wine, crushed garlic, cinnamon, salt and pepper. Put the remainder of oil to warm in a pan. Add the onions and the marinated meat. Cook for 1/2 hour, stirring from time to time. Add water if necessary. Add the crushed tomatoes and the ketchup. Simmer for 10 minutes. Check if meat is tender, otherwise add more water and let simmer further. Blend the flour, wine and sugar in a cup, add to meat in saucepan. Stir a few seconds more till the sauce thickens.

Fried green beans

Ingredients

500 g green beans, 1 pinch sodium bicarbonate, 1 crushed garlic clove,

1 tbsp butter, salt.

Preparation Remove the strings on the sides of the beans and boil them for half an hour with salt and sodium bicarbonate. Drain them in a strainer. Melt butter in a pan. Add crushed garlic and the beans. Fry and correct the seasoning if necessary.

Lettuce Salad (see P29)

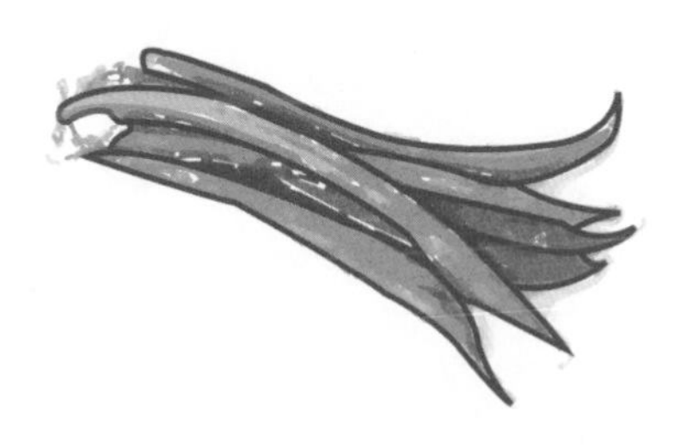

MORNING

Calebasse and dry shrimps curry

Ingredients

1 tender calebasse, 125 g dried shrimps, 1 chopped onion, 1/2 tsp crushed garlic, 1/2 tsp crushed ginger, 3 chopped tomatoes, 1 sprig curry leaves, 2 tbsp curry powder, 3 tbsp oil.

Preparation Peel the calebasse and cut in cubes. Put the shrimps to soak in hot water. Clean and wash in plenty of water. Heat oil in a saucepan. Add the pieces of onion, garlic, ginger, tomatoes, curry powder and the curry leaves. Add some water and allow to cook. Add the shrimps, calebasse, half cup of water and simmer for about 30 minutes on low heat by stirring from time to time. Switch off when calebasse is tender.

Cucumber salad

Ingredients

1 small cucumber, salt, 2 tsp vinegar, 1/2 tsp sugar, 4 small chillies.

Preparation Peel and remove the seeds part from the cucumber. Cut in thin strips. Pour a little boiling water on the strips of cucumber and drain it. Mix vinegar, sugar, salt and the chopped chillies. Add to the cucumber and mix well.

EVENING

Roasted chicken

Ingredients

1 whole chicken, salt, pepper, soy sauce.

Preparation Preheat oven at 180°C. Rub the chicken with soy sauce, salt and pepper and place into a baking dish. Put in the oven and cook for 45 minutes to 1 hour.

Courgettes à la sauce blanche

Ingredients

1 courgette, 1 tbsp flour, 1 tbsp butter, 1 cup milk, a piece of cheese, salt.

Preparation Cut the courgette in thin slices and allow to boil for 10 minutes. Drain them and place on a plate side by side to each other. Melt butter in a saucepan, add flour and mix well. Add milk, a little at a time, stirring well to prevent lump formation. Pour the white sauce on the slices of courgette. Sprinkle with grated cheese and brown under the grill.

MORNING

Red lentils

Ingredients

250 g red lentils, 1 sliced onion, 1/2 tsp crushed garlic, 1/2 tsp crushed ginger, salt, 2 tbsp oil, chopped coriander leaves.

Preparation Wash the lentils and soak for a few hours. Put in a pan with the sliced onion, garlic, ginger, salt, oil and 4 cups of water. Cook on low heat for 45 minutes. Garnish with coriander leaves.

Braised fish

Ingredients

4 fish slices, 6 crushed tomatoes, 1 thinly sliced onion, 1/2 tsp crushed garlic, 1/2 tsp crushed ginger, 1 tsp flour, 1 bunch coriander, 1/2 tsp sugar, salt, pepper, oil for frying.

Preparation Season fish with salt and pepper. Fry them in hot oil. Drain on absorbant paper. Heat oil in saucepan, add onion, garlic, ginger, tomatoes and salt. Cover and cook for a few minutes. Add fish to the sauce and simmer for a while. Blend the flour and sugar in some water. Pour on to fish and sprinkle with chopped coriander.

Fried margoze (Bittergourd)

Ingredients

500 g bittergourd, 1 thinly sliced onion, 1/2 tsp crushed garlic, 3 tbsp oil, salt.

Preparation Half the bittergourd lengthwise , empty them and slice thinly. Add a tbsp of salt. Rub the salt in thoroughly and allow to soak for 15 minutes. Wash the bittergourd with plenty of water to remove the salt. Heat oil in pan. Add onion, garlic and the bittergourd. Cook for about 15 minutes by stirring from time to time.

EVENING

Moussaka

Ingredients

1 kg medium egg-plant, 2 egg whites, oil, 500 g minced meat, 1 big chopped onion, 5 crushed tomatoes , 1/2 tsp crushed garlic, 2 tbsp ketchup, 1 tbsp flour, 1 tbsp butter, 1 cup milk, a slice cheese.

Preparation Cut the egg-plants in slices. Whisk the egg white with a fork, dip in the egg-plant in the egg and fry them in very hot oil. Drain on absorbant paper. Heat a little oil in a pan, add onion, garlic, minced meat, tomatoes and the ketchup. Cook till sauce thickens. Put a layer of fried egg-plants in a baking dish. Cover with a layer of the sauce. Alternate the egg-plants and the sauce by ending with a layer of sauce.

Preparing the white sauce:

Melt butter in a saucepan. Add flour and mix. Add the milk and stir well to prevent lumps forming. Pour the sauce on the tomato sauce. Sprinkle the grated cheese and grill before serving.

Lettuce Salad (see P29)

MORNING

Chicken chop suey

Ingredients

500 g chicken breast, 2 eggs, 1 small tin chinese sausage (optional), 2 carrots, 1 small chou-chou, 1/2 radish, 250 g chinese greens, 1 thinly sliced onion, 2 garlic cloves, 2 tbsp thinly chopped coriander, salt, pepper, 5 tbsp soy sauce, 1 tsp sugar, 2 tsp cornstarch, 2 tbsp white wine, oil.

Preparation Cut chicken breast into strips. Put them in a bowl with soy sauce, cornstarch, salt, pepper, crushed garlic and 2 tbsp oil. Marinate for 1/2 an hour. Slice carrots, chou-chou, radish into julienne. Bring to boil in a pan. Blanch the vegetables, each type at a time, in the water for a few seconds. Drain them in a strainer. Heat a little oil in wok. Add the chicken, stir fry on high heat, stirring well with a wooden spoon. Add the vegetables, onion, the Chinese sausages (optional) and the shredded greens and continue to stir. Cook for about 5 minutes on a low heat. Add the coriander, sugar, wine and cornstarch blended in water. Cook for a few more minutes and remove from heat. Make an omelette, cut in strips and place on top of the chop suey.

Potato Chutney (see P32)

EVENING

Gratin of potato and cod

Ingredients

1 kg potato, 500gm cod, 1/2 chopped onion, 1/2 tsp crushed garlic, 2 tbsp oil, 1 tbsp butter, 2 tbsp milk powder, 1 egg yolk, 1 slice of cheese, thyme, parsley, 3 tbsp breadcrumb.

Preparation

Put the potatoes and the cod to cook in a large pressure cooker (containing water) for nearly half an hour. When the potatoes are cooked, drain them, peel and mash them well with a fork. Remove the bones from the cod and flake it in a mixer. Heat oil in a saucepan, add onion, garlic, the cod and fry for a few seconds. Add the mashed potato, butter, milk, egg yolk, grated cheese, thyme, parsley and half cup of water. Stir with a wooden spoon so that the mixture does not stick. Check seasoning. Pour in a baking dish and sprinkle breadcrumbs. Grill before serving.

Cabbage salad

Ingredients

1 medium cabbage, 1/2 thinly sliced onion, 2 tbsp olive oil, 1/2 tbsp vinegar, 3 tbsp salad cream, salt, pepper.

Preparation

Shred the cabbage thinly. Mix oil, vinegar, salad cream, salt and pepper. Spoon the dressing over the cabbage and toss to mix before serving.

MORNING

Fricassée of pumpkin

Ingredients

1 kg pumpkin, 2 tbsp oil, 1 chopped onion, 1 tsp crushed garlic, 1/2 tsp crushed ginger, thyme, parsley, salt.

Preparation Peel and cut the pumpkin in cubes. Put the pieces of pumpkin in a saucepan with oil, onion, garlic, ginger, thyme, parsley and salt. Simmer on a gentle heat. Check cooking from time to time and add water if necessary. Check and correct seasoning.

Tuna in tomato sauce

Ingredients

1 can tuna (drained), 5 crushed tomatoes, 1/2 chopped onion, 1/2 tsp crushed garlic, 1/2 tsp crushed ginger, 2 tbsp oil, salt, 1 tbsp chopped parsley.

Preparation Heat oil in a saucepan. Add onion, garlic, ginger, tomatoes and salt. Cook for a few minutes before adding the tuna. Sprinkle wih chopped parsley.

Fried egg-plant

Ingredients

1 big egg-plant, 1 egg white, salt, pepper, oil for frying.

Preparation Wash egg-plant, dry it and cut into 1/2 cm thick slices. Beat the egg white, add salt and pepper. Dip the slices of egg-plant in the egg white and fry until they turn to a golden colour. Remove and drain on absorbant paper.

EVENING

Spanish rice

Ingredients

2 1/2 measures of white rice, 750 g chicken (skin removed), 1 small egg-plant, oil for frying, 2 tbsp oil, 1 tbsp butter, 2 sliced onion, 1 tsp cumin powder, 1/2 tsp crushed garlic, 1/2 tsp crushed ginger, 4 tomatoes, 1 tbsp tomato purée, 1 tbsp chopped parsley, salt.

Preparation Cut the chicken in pieces and remove the skin. Slice the egg-plant. Fry them. Remove and keep aside. Put 2 tbsp of oil and butter to warm in a saucepan. Add the onion and let cook a little. Put the cumin, garlic, ginger, the tomatoes, the tomato puree, salt and the pieces of chicken. Cook for 15 minutes by stirring from time to time. Wash the rice, put in the rice-cooker, add the chicken mixture as well as the slices of fried egg-plant and 3 measures of water. Switch on the rice-cooker and let cook. Before serving, sprinkle the chopped parsley.

Tomato Chutney (see P38)

MORNING

Pumpkin greens (brèdes) in bouillon

Ingredients

2 bunches of pumpkin greens, 1 tbsp oil, salt.

Preparation Clean the greens by taking care to remove the hard stems. Wash with plenty of water. Heat oil in a pan and add salt. Add 4 cups of water and let boil. At the first boil, put the bredes. Cover and let cook for about 10 minutes. Remove from heat and check seasoning.

Meat in tomato sauce

Ingredients

500 g meat (beef or lamb), 5 tomatoes, 1 onion, 3 tbsp oil, 1/2 tsp crushed garlic, 1/2 tsp crushed ginger, salt, pepper.

Preparation Cut the meat in cubes by taking care of removing the skin and tendons. Season. Chop onion and the tomatoes. Put oil to warm in a pan, add the pieces of onion and meat. Saute for a few minutes and add 1 cup of water. Let the meat cook well and add more water if necessary. Add garlic, ginger and the tomatoes. Add more water to allow the meat to cook completely. Heat oil in a pan. Add onion and meat. Brown for a few minutes and add 1 cup water. Cook until tender, adding more water if necessary. Add ginger, garlic, tomatoes and seasonings. Simmer until meat is thoroughly cooked.

Mango chutney

Ingredients

2 green mangoes, 1 onion, salt, 2 tsp oil, small green chillies to taste.

Preparation Peel and grate mangoes. Press well between the palms of the hands to remove excess juice. Slice onions. Mix the mangoes, sliced onion, salt, oil and the finely chopped green chillies.

EVENING

Vegetables salad with smoked marlin and croutons

Ingredients

500 g smoked marlin, 1 onion, 1 lettuce, 1 bunch watercress, 1 green apple, 1 avocado, 125 g sprouted mung beans, 1/2 can sweetcorn kernels, 6 green olives (pickled, stoned), 3 tbsp olive oil, 1 tbsp vinegar, 2 tbsp mayonnaise.

Preparation Clean and wash the lettuce, watercress and the sprouted mung beans. Cut the apple and the avocado in dice. Crumble the marlin. Cut the olives in two. Prepare a vinegar sauce by mixing oil, vinegar and the mayonnaise. Add the slice of chopped onion, the pieces of smoked marlin, apples, avocado, olives and the maize. Mix well. Add the lettuce, watercress and the sprouted mung beans before serving.

Croutons

Ingredients

2 slices loaf bread (one day old), oil for frying.

Preparation Cut the slices of bread in cubes. Fry in very hot oil until evenly browned. Scatter over the salad. Serve immediately.

Garlic bread

Ingredients

2 baguettes, 1/2 packet butter, 4 garlic cloves, 2 sprigs parsley, 1 pinch salt.

Preparation Peel and cut garlic cloves, wash the parsley. Put butter, garlic, parsley and salt in a mixer and blend thoroughly. Slice the baguettes at 5 cm interval by taking care of not cutting through each slice completely so that the bread remains in one piece. Spread each side of the cut with garlic butter. Make sure that each bread returns to its original shape and wrap them in aluminium foil. Cook in an oven at 180°C for 15 minutes.
Remove the aluminium foil before serving.

MORNING

Pork and egg-plant curry

Ingredients

1 kg pork, 2 long egg-plants, 1 big onion, 1/2 tsp crushed garlic, 1/2 tsp crushed ginger, 1 sprig curry leaves, 1 bunch coriander, 2 tsp of cumin powder, 3 tbsp curry powder, 4 tomatoes, 3 tbsp oil.

Preparation Remove all visible fat from the pork and cut into cubes. Cut the egg-plant lengthwise. Chop onion and tomatoes. Mix the curry powder and the cumin powder with some water to make a paste. Heat oil in a saucepan. Add onion, garlic, ginger and curry paste. Cook for one minute. Add the pieces of meat and the egg-plant and half cup of water, cook for a while and add the tomatoes and the curry leaves. Cover and simmer by stirring occasionally till the meat is tender and the pieces of egg-plant are reduced to a purée. Sprinkle chopped coriander and remove from heat.

Cucumber Salad (see P44)

EVENING

Vegetable soup with chicken or beef (see P16)

Bread stuffed with chicken

Ingredients

1 bread per person, 2 chicken breast, salt, pepper, 1 lettuce, 2 tomatoes, mayonnaise, mustard.

Preparation Season the chicken breast and cook in little water on a gentle heat. Cook thoroughly and slice thinly. Wash and drain lettuce. Slice tomatoes. Spread bread with mayonnaise and mustard. Place lettuce leaves, a slice of tomato, followed by the chicken. Put some more mayonnaise on the chicken. Serve.

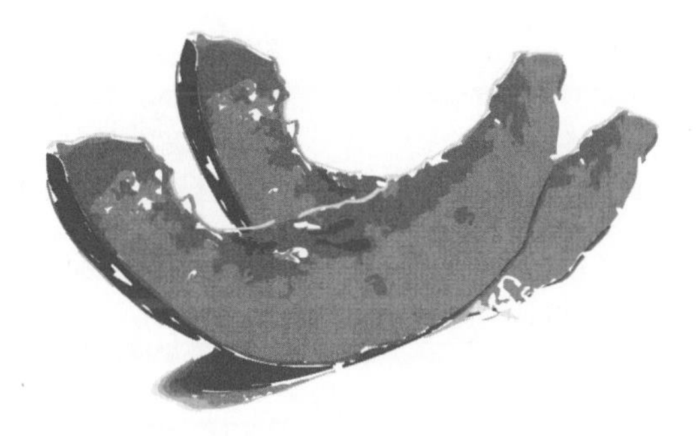

Menu 3

	Morning	Evening
Monday	Fricassée of vouèmes. Corned-beef in tomato sauce.	White fish in sauce. Watercress salad.
Tuesday	Pork with Chinese greens. Tomato chutney.	Chicken with mushrooms. Lettuce salad.
Wednesday	Pilau of beef with sausages. Tomato chutney.	Ham. Russian salad.
Thursday	Chicken stew and small peas. Cucumber salad.	Roast beef. Glazed carrots. Lettuce salad. Sauce mayonnaise.
Friday	Fricassée of butter beans. White salted fish in tomato sauce. Stewed brèdes malabar.	Fish fingers. Chips. Cabbage salad.
Saturday	Lamb curry. Tomato chutney.	Fried or grilled sausages. White sauce of cauliflower or carrots Lettuce salad.
Sunday	Stewed octopus. Vegetables relish	Meat pie. Lettuce salad.

The purchase list

Market

500 g vouèmes
1 bunch watercress
3 bunches chinese greens
1.5 kg potatoes
1 beetroot
1.5 kg carrots
1 cucumber
2 bunches of brèdes malabar
1 cabbage
1 cauliflower or 500 g carrots
1 tomato
4 lettuces
1 kg onions
2 kg tomatoes

125 g garlic
125 g ginger
2 bunches coriander
thyme
parsley
curry leaves
spring onions
green chillies

For vegetable pickles:
250 g cabbage
250 g carrots
250 g green beans
250 g small onions
green chillies

Supermarket

1.5 kg fish
500 g pork
2 whole chicken
500 g beef
1.5 kg beef
125 g creole sausage
1/2 packet of bacon
1 kg lamb
2 packets of chicken sausage
1.5 kg octopus
1 plate of chicken breast (500 g)

1 carton fish fingers
125 g ham
125 g white salted fish
1 can corned-beef
1 can mushrooms
1 can small peas
1 packet of butter beans
1 sachet spices "Pilau"
12 eggs
1 carton cheese "Cheddar" (500g)

MORNING

Fricassée of vouèmes

Ingredients

1/2 kg vouèmes, 1 chopped onion, 1/2 tsp crushed garlic, 1/2 tsp crushed ginger, 2 tomatoes coarsely chopped, 2 tbsp oil, salt.

Preparation Clean, wash and cut the vouèmes in small pieces. Heat oil in a pan, add onion, garlic and ginger. Sauté for a few seconds, add the vouèmes, tomatoes and salt. Add half-cup of water and cook by stirring occasionally.

Corned beef in tomato sauce

Ingredients

1 can corned beef, 5 tomatoes, 1 chopped onion, 1/2 tsp crushed garlic, 1/2 tsp crushed ginger, 1 sprig thyme, 2 tbsp oil.

Preparation Heat oil in a saucepan. Add onion, garlic and ginger, crushed tomatoes and the thyme. Sauté for a little while and add the corned beef. Cook for a few more minutes.

EVENING

Fish in béchamel sauce

Ingredients

1.5 kg fish, 1 tbsp butter, 1 onion, 1 sprig parsley, 1 sprig thyme, salt, pepper.

For the white sauce:

1 tbsp butter, 1 tbsp oil, 2 tbsp flour, 1 cup milk, 2 eggs.

Garnish:

2 boiled eggs, 1 tomato.

Preparation Put fish in a large frying pan with the onions cut into quarters, thyme, parsley, butter, salt and pepper. Add 2 cups water and cook on a slow heat. Check if the fish is done, remove from heat and allow to cool.

Preparation of white sauce:

Heat oil and butter in saucepan. Add the flour and stir. Add milk gradually, stirring continuously to avoid lumps. Add egg yolk and the beaten egg white. Mix well. Flake the fish in a plate by taking care of removing the bones. Pour the white sauce on the fish. Decorate with slices of tomato and eggs.

Watercress Salad (see P27)

MORNING

Chinese greens and pork

Ingredients

3 bunches Chinese greens, 500 g pork, 2 garlic cloves, 3 tbsp oil, 2 tbsp soy sauce, 1 tsp cornflour, salt, pepper.

Preparation Cut meat into cubes. Mix soy sauce, cornflour, pepper, crushed garlic and marinate for approximately 1 hour. Shred the greens. Heat oil in a wok. Add meat and stir fry. When the meat is done, add the greens and continue to stir until cooked but not too soft. Check seasoning and remove from heat.

Tomato chutney (see P38)

EVENING

Chicken with mushrooms

Ingredients

1 whole chicken, 1 can mushroom, 2 tbsp oil, 1 chopped onion, 1/2 tbsp crushed garlic, 1/2 tsp crushed ginger, 5 tomatoes crushed, 1 sprig thyme, 1 tbsp chopped parsley, salt, pepper.

Preparation Cut the chicken in pieces and remove all the skin and fat. Season with salt and pepper. Heat oil in a saucepan. Add the chicken and cook by stirring from time to time. When the chicken is almost cooked, remove from the saucepan and keep aside. In the same pan, add onions, garlic, ginger, thyme and tomatoes. Cook thoroughly. Add chicken and mushrooms cut in strips. Add water and cook on a slow heat. At the end of the cooking, sprinkle with chopped coriander.

Lettuce Salad (see P29)

MORNING

Beef pilau with sausage

Ingredients

2 1/2 measures (rice cooker) rice, 500 g beef, 250 g beef or chicken sausage, 1 big chopped onion, 1/2 tsp crushed garlic, 1/2 tsp crushed ginger, 2 tsp cumin powder, 1/2 sachet "Pilau spice-mix", 1 sprig curry leaves, 1 bunch chopped coriander, 1 tbsp butter, 3 chopped tomatoes, salt.

Preparation Cut the meat into cubes and separate the sausage. Cut the onion in quarters. Mix the cumin powder, the "Pilau" spice-mix in some water. Heat oil and butter in a saucepan and add the onions, garlic, ginger, tomatoes and salt. Sauté for a few seconds and add the mixed spices. Simmer for a few minutes more. Add meat and the sausage and cook for 25 minutes by stirring from time to time. In the meanwhile, wash the rice, put in the rice-cooker and drain away the water. Pour the spice mix and the meat over the rice. Add 3 1/2 cups of water, check the seasoning and switch on the rice-cooker. At the end of the cooking, use a fork to stir the rice carefully and sprinkle the chopped coriander.

Tomato chutney (see P38)

EVENING

Ham

Ingredients

Allow 2 slices of ham per person.

Russian salad

Ingredients

3 potatoes, 3 carrots, 1 beetroot, 2 eggs, 1 lettuce, 1 thinly sliced onion, 1 garlic clove, 3 tbsp olive oil, 1 tbsp vinegar, salt, pepper.

Preparation Put potatoes, carrots, beetroot and eggs to boil in a large pan with water and a little salt. Remove the potatoes first when they are tender, then the carrots and lastly the beetroot and eggs. Allow to cool and peel. Hull the eggs, cut in halves and remove the yolks. Thinly chop the egg white. Keep aside. Wash the lettuce. Prepare the vinaigrette by mixing the olive oil, vinegar, crushed garlic, salt, pepper and the thinly chopped egg white. Mix all the vegetables chopped in slices and the lettuce. Spoon the dressing over the salad and toss to mix just before serving. Serve with ham and bread.

MORNING

Braised chicken with small peas

Ingredients

1 whole chicken, 1 can peas, 1 chopped onion, 1/2 tsp crushed garlic, 1 sprig thyme, 1 tbsp chopped parsley, 3 chopped tomatoes, 1 tbsp flour, 2 tbsp oil, salt, pepper.

Preparation Cut the chicken into pieces. Season with salt and pepper and sprinkle with a little flour. Fry the chicken pieces in a non-stick saucepan. Heat oil in a pan. Add onion, garlic, thyme and tomatoes. Add chicken and 1 cup of water, cover, simmer until chicken is cooked. Stir in the drained peas and the parsley. Cook for a few minutes. Check seasoning.

Cucumber salad (see P44)

EVENING

Roast beef

Ingredients

1 1/2 kg beef, salt, pepper, 2 pieces cinnamon sticks, 10 cloves, 2 tbsp oil.

Preparation Clean beef by removing all the fatty parts. Put the meat and all remaining ingredients in a pressure cooker. Cover with water and let cook for half an hour until the moment hissing sound starts. Switch off. Allow the pressure to drop. Open the pressure cooker and cook without covering. Check the cooking from time to time. If all the water has evaporated and the meat is still not done, add more water till cooking is complete. Allow to cool down and cut in slices.

The cooking time cannot be given exactly, as this depends on size and tenderness of the meat joint.

Glazed carrots

Ingredients

1 kg carrots, 1 tbsp butter, 1/2 tsp sugar, salt, 1 tbsp chopped parsley.

Preparation Bring carrots to boil with salt. Allow to cool and peel. Cut lengthwise. Melt sugar in butter and add the carrots. Cook for a few seconds without breaking the carrots. Place on a plate and sprinkle with chopped parsley.

Mayonnaise

Ingredients

3 eggs, 1 garlic clove, 2 cups oil.

Preparation Boil one egg and allow to cool. Crush the garlic clove and the cooked yolk and transfer to a bowl. Add the remaining raw yolks and mix well. Pour oil little by little by beating continuously until all the oil is absorbed.

Lettuce Salad (see P29)

MORNING

Fricassée of butter beans

Ingredients

1 packet of butter beans, 1 1/2 litres water, 2 tbsp oil, 1 chopped onion, 1/2 tsp crushed garlic, 1/2 tsp crushed ginger, 1 sprig curry leaves, 1 tsp cumin powder, salt, 3 crushed tomatoes.

Preparation Wash the butter beans and soak for 5 to 6 hours. Put the beans and water to cook in a pressure cooker for 3/4 hour. Check cooking. Heat oil in a saucepan. Add the chopped onions, garlic, ginger, cumin powder, curry leaves, salt and tomatoes. Sauté for few minutes and add the butter beans. Sprinkle with chopped coriander.

White salted fish in tomato sauce

Ingredients

125 g salted white fish, 2 tbsp oil, 1 chopped onion, 1/2 tsp crushed garlic, 1/2 tsp crushed ginger, 5 tomatoes, chopped onion sprigs.

Preparation Bring salted fish to boil in 3 cups of water for 10 minutes. Wash with plenty of water and flake by taking care of removing the bones. Fry the salted fish in oil. Add the chopped onion, garlic, ginger and the tomatoes. Cook for a few moments and add the chopped onion sprigs. Check seasoning.

Braise of brèdes malabar

Ingredients

2 bunches brèdes malabar, 1 chopped onion, 1/2 tsp crushed garlic, 1/2 tsp crushed ginger, 1 tbsp oil, salt.

Preparation Clean the brèdes and wash in plenty of water. Heat oil in a saucepan. Add onion, garlic, ginger, a little salt and the brèdes. Cover the saucepan and let cook for about 15 minutes. Allow the water in the brèdes to dry.

EVENING

Fish Fingers

Ingredients

1 packet of Fish Fingers.

Preparation Put in a baking dish and bake for 30 minutes approximately, just before serving.

Chips

Ingredients

1 kg potatoes, oil for frying, salt, pepper.

Preparation Peel the potatoes and cut them in 1/2 cm cube sticks. Wash and wipe them dry. Heat oil in a frying pan and dip in the chips. Stir very often. Remove the chips when they reach a golden colour and place on absorbant paper. Season with salt and pepper. Repeat this exercise again till all chips are fried.

Cabbage Salad (see P49)

MORNING

Lamb curry

Ingredients

1 kg lamb, 2 potatoes, 3 crushed tomatoes, 1 chopped onion, 1/2 tsp crushed garlic, 1/2 tsp crushed ginger, 1 sprig curry leaves, 3 tbsp curry powder, 1 tsp cumin powder, 1/2 bunch coriander, salt, pepper, 4 tbsp oil.

Preparation Cut the meat into cubes and marinate for 10 minutes with salt, pepper and 1 tbsp of oil. Cut the potatoes into cubes. Prepare a paste with the curry powder, cumin powder and a little water. Heat oil in a saucepan. Add onion, garlic, ginger, curry mix and the tomatoes. Cook for a few minutes before adding the pieces of lamb and potatoes as well as the curry leaves. Cook for about 20 minutes by adding water from time to time if necessary. Check the cooking and seasoning. Garnish with chopped coriander.

Tomato chutney (see P38)

EVENING

Fried sausages (or grilled)

Ingredients

2 packets of sausages of your choice, oil for frying.

Preparation Allow the sausages to thaw completely and fry them. You can also grill them.

Cauliflower or carrots in white sauce

Ingredients

1 cauliflower or 500 g of carrots, 1 tbsp flour, 1 tbsp butter, 1 cup milk, a piece cheese, salt.

Preparation Cut the cauliflower into florets or the carrots into cubes and boil them till they are tender. Drain and set aside. Melt butter in a saucepan. Add flour and mix. Add milk and stir well to avoid lumps. Add the vegetables to the white sauce, mix well and let cook a little more. Spoon the mixture in a baking dish. Sprinkle with grated cheese and brown under the grill.

Lettuce Salad (see P29)

MORNING

Braised octopus

Ingredients

1.5 kg octopus, 1 chopped onion, 1/2 tsp crushed garlic, 1/2 tsp crushed ginger, 1 sprig thyme, 5 chopped tomatoes, 1 tsp cinnamon, salt, 1 tsp cornflour, 3 tbsp oil.

Preparation The octopus must be very clean. Cook in 1 litre of water in a pressure cooker for 45 minutes till the hissing sound starts. Reduce pressure, then open the pan to check whether the octopus is tender. If not, cook for another 15 minutes by adding water if necessary. When the octopus is well cooked, wash it to remove all the small black skin, which remains on the tentacles. Cut them in small pieces. Heat oil, add onion, garlic, ginger, thyme and the pieces of octopus. Sauté for a few moments and add the tomatoes and cinnamon. Pour 1/2 cup of water, cover the saucepan and let simmer for 5 minutes. Add salt. Dilute the cornflour in water and mix with the preparation. Stir till the sauce thickens. Check seasoning.

Vegetable relish (see P8)

EVENING

Meat pie

Ingredients for the pastry

300 g flour, 100 g butter, 2 tbsp oil, 1/2 cup water, 1 egg yolk.

Ingredients for the filling

500 g chicken breast, 1 big white onion, 1 sprig thyme, 1 tsp chopped parsley, salt, pepper, 1 piece of stale bread, 2 tbsp oil, 1 egg, 1 boiled egg.

Preparation Pastry: Mix all the ingredients and knead to make a dough. Let it rest in the fridge for 30 minutes.

Filling: Chop the breast chicken. Thinly chop the onion. Put the stale bread to soak and drain well. Sauté the chopped chicken in hot oil with salt and pepper. Add onion, thyme, the parsley, soaked bread and the whole egg. Let the water dry and cool down. Check seasoning. Turn the dough on to a floured surface, knead and roll lightly to the width of 30 cm by 30 cm. Spread the filling in the middle of the pastry. Spoon in the hardboiled egg in the middle of the filling. Fold the border of the paste so that it is well sealed. Press well on each side. Brush the pastry with the yolk. Bake in a preheated oven for about one hour at 180°C.

Lettuce Salad (see P29)

Menu 4

	Morning	Evening
Monday	Fish in bouillon. Braised lady finger. Coconut chutney.	Mixed vegetable and sausages. Lettuce salad.
Tuesday	Chinese noodle. Garlic sauce.	Tuna quiche. Lettuce salad.
Wednesday	Braised cabbage and tanned. Coriander chutney.	Lamb ragout. Lettuce salad.
Thursday	Egg plant curry and dry shrimps. Tomato chutney.	Spaghetti Bolognese with grated 'Parmesan' cheese.
Friday	Pumpkin fricassee. Braised fish.	Mashed potatoes and corned-beef. Lettuce salad.
Saturday	Dhal. White salted fish in tomato sauce.	Barbecue. Salad.
Sunday	Venison and embrevades curry. Tomato chutney.	Omelet with ham. Lettuce salad.

The purchase list

Market

500 g ladyfinger
1.5 kg potatoes
500 g carrots
2 leeks
2 cabbages
1 kg eggplant
1 kg pumpkin
1 chou-chou
1 beetroot
2 pâtissons

5 tomatoes
250 g embrevades
1 bunch watercress
2 kg tomatoes
1 kg onions
125 g garlic
125 g ginger
3 bunches coriander
2 pieces coconut
3 sprigs curry leaves

1 bunch mint
1 bunch onion springs
chillies
thyme
parsley
2 packets of chinese noodles
1 lettuce

Supermarket

1 kg fish
750 g fish fillet
1 packet sausage
2 trays minced meat
1 kg lamb
1 kg venison
Meat of your choice
for the BBQ

3 slices ham
125 g tanned
125 g dry crayfish
250 g salted white fish
1 can tuna
1 can corned beef
2 cans tomato purée
2 cans mushrooms

250 g split peas (dhal)
1 packet spaghetti
12 eggs
1 piece of 'Parmesan'
cheese
2 cartons cheese "Cheddar"
(2 x 250 g)

MORNING

Fish in bouillon

Ingredients

1 kg fish (of your choice), scaled and sliced, 1 chopped onion, 1/2 tsp crushed garlic, 1/2 tsp crushed ginger, 1 sprig thyme, 3 crushed tomatoes, salt, pepper, 1 tsp chopped coriander, 1/2 cup oil.

Preparation Season fish with salt and pepper. Fry them and place on absorbant paper. Heat 2 tbsp of oil. Add onions, garlic, ginger, thyme and tomatoes. Cook for 2-3 minutes and add 5 cups of water. Boil for about 15 minutes nearly. Add the slices of fish and simmer for 10 minutes. Sprinkle chopped coriander.

Braised lady finger

Ingredients

500 g ladyfingers, 2 tomatoes (diced), 1 chopped onion, 1/2 tsp crushed garlic, 1/2 tsp crushed ginger, 3 tbsp oil, salt.

Preparation Wash the ladyfingers. Cut the tail and stalks. Heat oil. Add onion, garlic, ginger and salt. Sauté for a few seconds. Add the ladyfingers and tomatoes. Simmer for 5 minutes and add 1 cup of water. Cook on small fire till water is reduced.

Coconut chutney (see P42)

EVENING

Mixed vegetables with sausages

Ingredients

1 packet sausages, 1 big potato, 2 carrots, 2 leeks, 1/4 cabbage, 1 onion, 2 garlic cloves, 3 tomatoes, thyme, parsley, 1 tbsp butter, 3 tbsp oil, salt.

Preparation Peel and dice potato and carrots. Chop the leeks thinly and shred the cabbage thickly. Chop onion and garlic cloves. Crush tomatoes. Fry the sausages and place on absorbant paper. In the same oil, add butter, onion, garlic, thyme, tomatoes, salt and the vegetables. Cover and cook for a few minutes. Add 2 cups of water and continue cooking. Check from time to time if water is completely reduced. The vegetables must be well cooked and a little sauce left. At the end of cooking, sprinkle the chopped parsley.

Lettuce Salad (see P29)

MORNING

Chinese noodles

Ingredients

2 packets of fresh chinese noodles, 6 tbsp soy sauce, 500 g minced beef, 1 bunch spring onion, 2 garlic cloves, 1 tsp sugar, 2 tbsp oil, salt, pepper.

Preparation Chop garlic and spring onion. Heat oil in a wok. Add garlic, minced meat and pepper. Cook the meat thoroughly. Add soy sauce and the noodles. Stir well. Add the spring onion and sugar. Check seasoning.

Garlic sauce

Ingredients

1 garlic clove, 3 tbsp vinegar, 3 tbsp water, 1/2 tsp sugar, 1 tsp chopped coriander, salt, 3 big green chillies.

Preparation Crush garlic and chillies with salt in a mixer. Put in a bowl. Add vinegar, water, sugar and coriander. Mix well.

EVENING

Tuna quiche

Ingredients for the pastry

300 g flour, 125 g butter, 1 egg yolk, salt, 1/2 cup water.

Ingredients for the filling

1 can tuna, 2 big white onion, 1 tbsp flour, 2 tbsp butter,
2 whole eggs, 1 cup milk, 1 piece of cheese, salt, pepper.

Preparation Preparing the pastry: Mix all ingredients, turn the dough on to a lightly floured surface and knead lightly to form a ball. Leave aside for half an hour.

Preparing the filling: Peel and slice onions into rings. Heat 1 tbsp butter. Sauté the onions and add the drained tuna. Put aside. In another saucepan, melt 1 tbsp butter. Add flour and mix well. Add milk gradually stirring well to prevent lumps. Stir in the tuna mixture and mix well. Add eggs and stir vigorously. Season with salt and pepper. Roll out dough and push in an oiled tin. Prick the base with a fork. Fill the pastry case with the filling mixture and sprinkle with the grated cheese. Put in a pre-heated oven at 180°C and bake for 45 minutes.

Lettuce Salad (see P29)

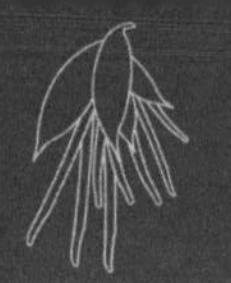

MORNING

Braised cabbage and tanned

Ingredients

1 cabbage, 250 g of tanned (smoked breast), 2 cloves, 3 chopped tomatoes, 1 chopped onion, 1/2 tsp crushed garlic, 1/2 tsp crushed ginger, salt, pepper, 2 tsp oil, 1/2 tsp sugar.

Preparation Boil the tanned in 3 cups of water. Cut the cabbage roughly and wash with plenty of water. When the tanned is very tender, remove the water. Cut in slice pieces. Warm oil in a saucepan. Add onion, garlic, ginger, the tanned pieces, salt, pepper, cloves, tomatoes and the cabbage. Cover and simmer gently on low heat. Stir from time to time. Let the water dry. Add sugar at the end of the cooking.

Coriander chutney (see P28)

EVENING

Ragout of lamb

Ingredients

1 kg lamb, 2 big onions (sliced into rings), 1/2 glass red wine, 2 garlic cloves, 2 tsp cinnamon powder, 4 cloves, 5 tomatoes, 2 tbsp tomato purée, 1 tbsp butter, 3 tbsp oil, salt, pepper, thyme, parsley, 1/2 tsp sugar, 1 tsp cornstarch.

Preparation Clean the lamb and cut into cubes. Season with salt and pepper. Add wine, 1 onion, crushed garlic, cinnamon and cloves. Marinate for 2 hours. Heat oil in a saucepan. Add the remaining onion and the thyme. Pour the meat and all the marinade. Cover and cook on high heat for about 10 minutes. Add 3 cups of water and reduce the heat. Cook for about 30 minutes more. Crush the tomatoes and mix with the tomato purée. Add to the saucepan. Check if the meat is tender and add water if necessary. Blend the cornstarch and sugar in some water and add in the saucepan. Add butter and sprinkle with chopped parsley.

Lettuce Salad (see P29)

MORNING

Egg-plant and dried shrimps curry

Ingredients

750 g egg-plants, 125 g dried shrimps, 1 chopped onion, 1/2 tsp crushed garlic, 1/2 tsp crushed ginger, 1 sprig curry leaves, 2 tbsp curry powder, 3 chopped tomatoes, 1 bunch coriander, salt, 2 tbsp oil.

Preparation Cut the egg-plants into cubes and soak in a bowl of water. Put the dried shrimps to soak in boiling water for about 15 minutes. Heat oil in a saucepan. Add onion and the drained shrimps, cook for a while and add the curry powder, tomatoes, salt, curry leaves, garlic, ginger, eggplants and 1/2 cup water. Cover and let simmer. Check cooking and seasoning. Sprinkle with chopped coriander.

Tomato chutney (see P38)

EVENING

Spaghetti Bolognese

Ingredients

1 packet of spaghetti, 500 g minced meat, 1/2 can mushrooms thinly sliced, 1 can tomato purée, 5 tomatoes, 1 onion (thinly chopped), thyme, chopped parsley, 1/2 tsp crushed garlic, salt, pepper, 4 tbsp oil.

Preparation Bring a large pan of water to boil with a little salt and 2 tbsp of oil. As the water starts to boil, add the spaghetti. Stir from time to time with a fork. Check cooking very often. As soon as the spaghetti is cooked, drain and wash with cold water. Heat 2 tbsp of oil in a saucepan. Add onion, garlic, chopped meat, salt and pepper. Sauté for a while. Add the mushroom, thyme, crushed tomatoes, tomato purée and 1/4 cup of water. Cook for about 15 minutes. Check seasoning and sprinkle with chopped parsley. Put spaghetti in a large soup plate and pour the meat sauce on it. Sprinkle with chopped parsley. You can accompany this menu with thinly grated Parmesan cheese, served separately.

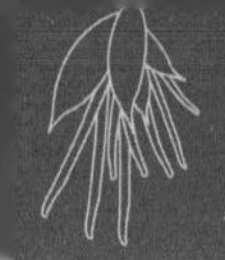

MORNING

Fricassée of pumpkin (see P50)

Braised fish (see P46)

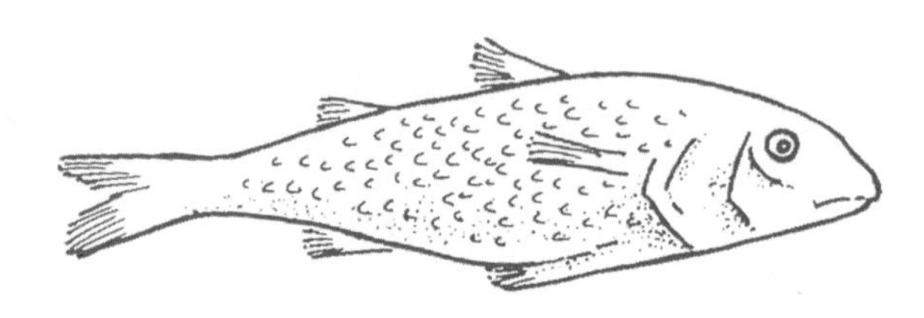

EVENING

Mashed potatoes with corned beef

Ingredients

750 g potatoes, salt, 4 tbsp powdered milk, 1 tbsp butter, 1 eggyolk, 1 can corned beef, 1/2 sliced onion, 1/2 tsp crushed garlic, 3 crushed tomatoes, 2 tbsp oil, breadcrumb.

Preparation Peel the potatoes, cut into cubes and boil them in plenty of water with salt. In the meantime, in another saucepan, heat oil, add onion, garlic and tomatoes. Cook for a while and add the corned beef. Mix well and cook for a few more minutes. Remove from heat and check seasoning. Pour this preparation in a soup plate. When the potatoes are ready, drain and crush them with a fork. Add milk, butter, the eggyolk and water if necessary. Check seasoning and cook for a few more minutes. Add this purée onto the corned beef mixture. Sprinkle breadcrumbs on top and brown in the oven at 180°C.

Lettuce Salad (see P29)

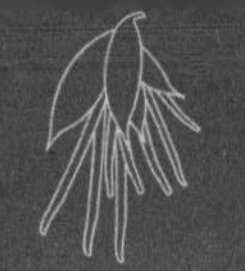

MORNING

Dhal curry

Ingredients

250 g dhal (split peas), 2 small eggplants, 1 chou-chou, 1/2 thinly chopped onion, 2 chopped tomatoes, 1/2 tsp crushed garlic, 1/2 tsp crushed ginger, 1 sprig curry leaves, 2 tsp curry powder, 1 tbsp oil, salt, 1 tsp cumin powder.

Preparation Wash the split peas and cook in a pressure cooker with the chou-chou cut into dice, the eggplant sliced length wise, 1 tsp salt and 1 1/2 litres water for 40 minutes. Heat oil in a saucepan. Add onion, curry powder, tomatoes, garlic, ginger, the curry leaves and the cumin powder. Stir well and add the dhal peas. Simmer for about 10 minutes. Check seasoning.

White salted fish in tomato sauce

Ingredients

250 g white salted fish, 5 crushed tomatoes, 1 chopped onion, 1/2 tsp crushed garlic, 1/2 tsp crushed ginger, salt, 2 tbsp oil.

Preparation Boil the salted fish. Drain water and put under cold water. Flake fish. Heat oil in a pan. Fry the flaked salted fish. Remove the salted fish and keep aside. In the same saucepan, add onion, garlic, ginger and the tomatoes (crushed in a mixer if possible). Add a little water and let cook for a few minutes. Then add the fried salted fish and simmer for some more minutes.

EVENING

Barbecue

Ingredients

Different types of meat, soy sauce, honey, sugar, salt, pepper or other sauces to marinate.

Preparation Marinate the meat for half a day. In the evening, switch on the BBQ set and let cook the meat.

Raw vegetables salad

Ingredients

3 carrots, 1 beetroot, 2 squash, 5 tomatoes

Preparation Grate the carrots, beetroot and squash. Slice tomatoes . Put all the vegetables side by side in a large plate. Pour a little dressing (see below vinaigrette) on the raw vegetables before serving.

Potato salad

Ingredients

5 potatoes, 2 tbsp mayonnaise, salt, pepper, thyme, parsley.

Preparation Wash, peel and boil the potatoes. Cut them in cubes and mix with the mayonnaise. Add salt, pepper and the thinly chopped herbs. Mix well.

Vinaigrette

Ingredients

2 tbsp olive oil, 1/2 tbsp vinegar, 1/2 tsp mustard paste, salt, pepper.

Preparation Mix oil, vinegar, mustard, salt and pepper.

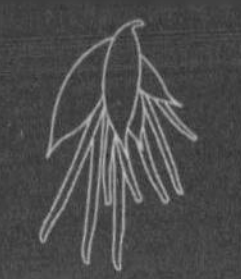

MORNING

Venison and embrevades curry

Ingredients

1 kg boneless venison, 4 tbsp oil, 1/2 lb embrevades peas, 1 chopped onion, 1/2 tsp crushed garlic, 1/2 tsp crushed ginger, 4 tbsp curry powder, 2 tsp cumin powder, 1 sprig curry leaves, 1/2 bunch coriander, 4 chopped tomatoes, salt, pepper.

Preparation Cut the venison in small pieces. Marinate for half an hour with salt, pepper and 2 tbsp of oil. In the meanwhile, blanch the embrevades and drain them. Mix the curry powder and the cumin with a little water to make a paste. Heat 2 tbsp of oil in a saucepan. Add onion, garlic, ginger and the curry paste. Sauté and add the meat, tomatoes, curry leaves and simmer on a gentle heat. Check the cooking from time to time and add water if the curry gets too dry. Add the embrevades, a little water and cook for a few more minutes. Chop the coriander and add to the curry at the end of the cooking.

Tomato chutney (see P38)

EVENING

Omelet with ham

Ingredients

6 eggs, 3 slices of ham, 1 can mushrooms, 1 onion, 1 sprig parsley, 1 piece of cheese, 2 tbsp oil, salt, pepper.

Preparation Cut the slices of ham in small pieces. Slice the mushrooms thinly. Chop onion and parsley thinly. Grate cheese. Beat 3 eggs and mix half of the ingredients, salt and pepper. Mix well. Put 1 tbsp of oil in a non-stick frying pan and pour the egg mixture. Turn the omelette and let it cook on the two sides. Repeat with the remaining eggs.

Lettuce Salad (see P29)

Index

Index

Index